Dominie
Chapter
Books

My Family & the Wasps

By John Parker
Illustrated by Edward Mooney

꜒ Dominie Press, Inc.

Publisher: Raymond Yuen
Editor: Bob Rowland
Designer: Mark Deutman
Illustrator: Edward Mooney
Cover Deisgner: Carol Anne Craft

Published by:

௵ Dominie Press, Inc.
1949 Kellogg Avenue
Carlsbad, California 92008 USA

ISBN 0-7685-0318-3

Printed in Singapore by PH Productions Pte Ltd

3 4 5 6 IP 05 04 03 02

TABLE OF CONTENTS

☆ ☆ ☆ ☆ ☆ ☆ ☆ ☆ ☆ ☆ ☆ ☆ ☆ ☆

Cast of Characters

Maxie the dog . . . . Narrator

Sneakers . . . . Maxie's "owner"

Food . . . . Mom

Deep Voice . . . . Dad

☆ ☆ ☆ ☆ ☆ ☆ ☆ ☆ ☆ ☆ ☆ ☆ ☆ ☆

Chapter One
A Nest of Wasps!

Sneakers was throwing a tennis ball for me to catch.

"Try this one, doggie-woggie!" he squeaked.

But he overdid it. The ball slipped out of his hand and landed on the roof. It bounced twice, and then rolled into the rain gutter that lined the roof. Lost, I hoped. After all, what sensible dog wants to chase a ball after lunch?

"No more ball-ball for Maxie," said *Sneakers*. He talks to me like that because he's still in the puppy stage. You see, I only play ball to give *Sneakers* something to do. But I whimpered a little just to please him.

"Me get ball-ball for good doggie," said *Sneakers*.

Then he ran off, while I kept an urgent appointment with an itch behind my right ear. Within a few minutes, he returned with a ladder.

"Soon have nice ball for play-play," said *Sneakers*.

"No hurry," I thought. But just to please him, I woofed a loud woof, did one or two dance steps, and wagged the old tail.

I had *Sneakers* well-trained. He climbed up that
ladder as if there were a juicy steak at the top. But at
the top, he didn't reach out for the tennis ball.
Instead, he waved his legs—sorry, I mean arms—as if
he were trying to shoo something away. And he
came down the ladder twice as fast as he went up.

He ran over to *Food* and shouted, "Mom!
There's a wasps' nest on the roof! And
thousands of wasps!"

"Don't exaggerate, *Sneakers*," I said to myself.
But he only became more excited.

"Millions of red-and-black wasps with long legs," he said. "They buzzed all around me. And they're angry!"

Food put her paw—sorry, I mean her hand—over her mouth and let out a little scream.

"Oh, dear! A wasps' nest!" she said.

"No need to get so excited," I thought. "I could have told you there was a wasps' nest up there if you had asked me." We dogs know these things.

"Trillions of them, Mom!" said *Sneakers*, exaggerating even more.

I was investigating an itch behind my left ear when *Deep Voice* came out from the garage, wondering what all the fuss was about. He had a rag and a small can of polish in his hand. As usual on a Saturday afternoon, he was scrubbing and rubbing that four-wheeled machine of his. If I rubbed myself that much, I would have disappeared a long time ago!

Deep Voice wasn't too worried about the wasps.

"A wasps' nest?" he said to *Food* and *Sneakers*.
"Is that all? I thought maybe we'd been invaded by
aliens from outer space!"

A big laugh rumbled from his chest.

"No problem," he said. "One or two squirts of
bug spray will fix them."

Deep Voice reached into the cupboard in the garage and found a big can of bug spray. He went back outside and held the can steady in one hand while he climbed the ladder.

But when he got to the top, his arms waved in the
air even more than *Sneakers'*. In fact, *Deep Voice*
looked like a traffic cop in the middle of rush hour.

His arms were still waving as he hurtled down the ladder. I suppose that was why he tripped on the bottom rung and fell flat on his back.

"Ow!" yelled *Deep Voice*.

I wagged my tail. Little events like that help the day go faster.

Deep Voice picked himself up while *Food* picked up the bug spray and fussed over him.

"I'll wait until it's cooler," said *Deep Voice*, rubbing his sore spots. "Those wasps get excited when it's hot."

Sneakers turned to me and rubbed my ears.

"Wasps, Maxie! Exciting, Maxie! Good doggie-woggie!"

I decided to take a nap before dinner.

Chapter Two

Dad Fights Back with Bug Spray

During dinner, I noticed that, as usual, *Food* gave me only one helping of my food. But she gave two helpings of their food to *Deep Voice* and *Sneakers*. And their helpings were enormous! My helping was pitiful. You could scarcely see it. Two licks and a gulp, and it was all gone. But I don't complain. It's a dog's life.

After dinner, *Deep Voice* went up the ladder again. He stopped when he was half-way to the top.

"The wind is blowing in my face," he shouted. "The bug spray might get in my eyes."

Food turned to *Sneakers*. "Get Dad's goggles," she said. "They're in the bottom cupboard in the garage."

I went with *Sneakers* to the garage. An ordinary dog would have stayed in the yard. But I'm not like that. I wanted to keep him safe. And it's a good thing I went with him. When *Sneakers* opened the cupboard, all sorts of odds and ends fell out. And in the confusion, half a chocolate bar fell out of his jacket pocket.

Well, would you believe that Sneakers was about to eat that chocolate?! It was five weeks old! It might have upset his stomach!

I had to act quickly–and I did. I licked up that chocolate and ate it before *Sneakers* could. When I think about it, I blush at my bravery and heroism. It's just another example of why I'm man's best friend.

Sneakers understood my noble act. He gave me a well-deserved pat on the head before he went back outside and handed the goggles to *Deep Voice*.

Deep Voice put on the goggles and climbed that ladder. I was pleased that he was getting plenty of exercise. Soon I wouldn't have to take him for a walk.

This time, *Deep Voice* climbed almost to the top
of the ladder. But he stopped when *Food* said
something to him.

"What if the wasps sting you on the hands,"
she said.

I could see that *Deep Voice* was thinking that stings on his hand would be even worse than falling off the ladder and hurting his tail–I mean his back.

"I'd better put on my garden gloves," he said.

"And I think I'd better hurry before it gets dark."

So *Sneakers* ran down to the cupboard in the garage again. I went, too, to search for dangerous chocolate bars. Unluckily—I mean luckily—we didn't find any. But we *did* find the garden gloves. There were a few rips in them, and the gloves smelled like rotting leaves, but they were better than nothing.

Deep Voice pulled on the gloves and started
climbing up the ladder. I knew it was going to
happen–*Food* stopped him again.

"What if those nasty things sting your nose?" she
said. "When that happened to Aunt Judy, her nose
swelled up like a football for weeks."

Deep Voice was thinking deep thoughts about his nose. He didn't want it to look like *any* kind of ball, even a ball as small as that tennis ball caught in the rain gutter. Of course, the real trouble with *Deep Voice's* nose was that it wasn't wet, black, and furry. But you can't expect everything of people. Even I'm not perfect.

Sneakers ran into the garage again. This time I stayed outside with *Deep Voice* and *Food*. I knew there were no more dangerous chocolate bars in the garage. In a few minutes, *Sneakers* returned with an old brown woolen scarf. It looked like something I wouldn't even sleep on. And it smelled like a moldy rag. But *Deep Voice* put it on his face. Now he looked like a burglar or a bank robber.

Up the ladder he went. But he didn't get to the
top this time, either. He stopped and said something
through that moldy scarf.

"Muff wuff! Guff wuff! Pluff wuff!"

"What?" shouted *Food* and *Sneakers*.

They should have asked me what he wanted. It
was getting dark. *Deep Voice* couldn't see very well.

So *Food* went into the kitchen to get a flashlight. I went, too. You never know. There might be some dangerous little snacks in the refrigerator. In which case, of course, I would eat them and sacrifice myself for the rest of the family. There were no dangerous snacks, but there *was* a fly swatter and a flashlight.

Food brought the fly swatter and the flashlight
outside, where *Deep Voice* and *Sneakers* were waiting.
Deep Voice held the flashlight and the fly swatter in
one hand. He held the bug spray in the other hand.
And up the ladder he went. It was tricky, because he
had so much to balance. But he did it. I was proud of
him. This time, he made it all the way to the top.

"Careful, dear," said *Food*.

"Campf fee sing umph eer!" *Deep Voice* said through the moldy scarf. I knew what that meant. We dogs know these things. It meant, "I can't see a thing up here!"

Sneakers held his breath. *Deep Voice* was about to zap the wasps!

Just then, I saw the bright yellow beam of a flashlight. The only trouble was, the flashlight belonged to someone else.

Chapter Three

A Crashing Defeat

"Police!" shouted the people behind the beam of light.

"Come down from that ladder! Hands in the air!"

Deep Voice jerked his head around in shock. He got the full force of the flashlight in his eyes.

41

I snarled under my breath and let out a nasty-sounding bark–just to let the police know they'd better watch their step.

Deep Voice's head jerked around the other way. That did it–the ladder began to slip.

"Aaaaaaah!" yelled *Deep Voice,* in a very loud, high voice. He waved his arms wildly as he tried to keep his balance. But it didn't do any good. The ladder slipped faster and faster, with *Deep Voice* still shouting at the top.

The ladder crashed into the bushes with a loud thump. *Food* screamed.

"Are you alright, Dad?" asked *Sneakers*.

"Pluff pliff!" answered *Deep Voice*. And then he scrambled out from the bushes. He was covered with leaves and dirt. His goggles were hanging off one ear, and his scarf was twisted over his nose.

Deep Voice ripped off his scarf and tried to explain things to the police. Then there was a loud clattering sound from the roof. It was the can of bug spray. And two seconds later, it landed on his head.

THUMP!

"Ow!" said *Deep Voice.*

That was when *Food* and *Sneakers* started laughing. They tried not to laugh, but they couldn't help it.

Food explained everything to the police. Then she made a cup of strong coffee for *Deep Voice*. He went to bed later with a headache.

Chapter Four

All's Well That Ends Well

Sneakers tried to comfort me about the lost ball. "Poor doggie-woggie."

"Hurray!" I thought. But still I looked at him sadly. Great tactic! *Sneakers* gave me a juicy dog biscuit to cheer me up.

As for that wasps' nest, *Sneakers* went up the ladder the next day to have a look at it. When he came back down, he had good news and bad news. The good news was that all the wasps had disappeared. The nest was empty. *Deep Voice* thought he had gotten rid of them, but I think they left for some peace and quiet. We dogs know these things.

The bad news? *Sneakers* found that tennis ball.

Oh well. I'd better wag my tail and pretend that I like to play ball with him. At least it gives *Sneakers* a little exercise.